better together*

* This book is best read together, grownup and kid.

 **akidsco.com**

a kids
book
about

a kids book about

EXECUTIVE FUNCTIONING

by Iris Wong

A Kids Co.
Editor Emma Wolf
Designer Rick DeLucco
Creative Director Rick DeLucco
Studio Manager Kenya Feldes
Sales Director Melanie Wilkins
Head of Books Jennifer Goldstein
CEO and Founder Jelani Memory

DK
Delhi Technical Team Bimlesh Tiwary Pushpak Tyagi, Rakesh Kumar
Senior Production Editor Jennifer Murray
Senior Production Controller Louise Minihane
Senior Acquisitions Editor Katy Flint
Acquisitions Project Editor Sara Forster
Managing Art Editor Vicky Short
Managing Director, Licensing Mark Searle

First American edition, 2025
Published in the United States by DK Publishing, 1745 Broadway, 20ᵗʰ Floor,
New York, NY 10019

First published in Great Britain in 2025 by
Dorling Kindersley Limited, 20 Vauxhall Bridge Road, London SW1V 2SA
A Penguin Random House Company

The authorised representative in the EEA is
Dorling Kindersley Verlag GmbH. Arnulfstr. 124, 80636 Munich, Germany

A catalog record for this book is available from the Library of Congress.
A CIP catalogue record for this book is available from the British Library.
ISBN: 978-0-2417-4376-8

DK books are available at special discounts when purchased in bulk for sales
promotions, premiums, fund-raising, or education use. For details, contact:
DK Publishing Special Markets, 1745 Broadway, 20th Floor, New York, NY 10019
SpecialSales@dk.com

Printed and bound in China
www.dk.com
akidsco.com

MIX
Paper | Supporting
responsible forestry
FSC™ C018179

This book was made with Forest
Stewardship Council™ certified
paper – one small step in DK's
commitment to a sustainable future.
**Learn more at www.dk.com/uk/
information/sustainability**

To Warren, Atticus, and Imogen.

To my past (and future) students.

To kids (and the kid in each of us) of all neurotypes!

Intro
for grownups

Hello, grownups! I'm so glad you're here. And there's something big I want you to know: the brain develops from the bottom up. That means that executive functioning (EF) is the last major brain center to develop. It's housed in the frontal lobe.

Our brains begin to develop the ability to connect mental and physical action at birth...that's what EF is! Growth spurts, which push our brains to make clearer connections, then arrive via neural pruning (like garden pruning)—when we are in preschool, and then before our teens. As EF is "late-developing," our brain continues to consolidate and organize well into our mid-20s. Mind blown, anyone?

This could be a wake-up call for us to recalibrate expectations. For ourselves. For the people we live or work with. For our kids.

What if we saw behavior as communication?

Is the person in front of us...tired? Burned out? Overstimulated? Distracted? Hungry? Trying really hard on the inside (when it's hard to see on the outside)? Masking feeling overwhelmed?

I have more to say, but first, join me in this book. See you on the flip side!

EVERYONE HAS A BODY AND BRAIN.

I just did some
reflexive questioning with you.

That's grownup speak for asking
you questions that make you
think about your thinking.

So anyway, back to brains and bodies.

Your brain tells your body what to...

DO, THINK, AND FEEL.

Hey, that has a name!

It's long. Brace yourself...

EXECU
FUNCTI

TIVE
ONING!

Did it spill off the page
and into your lap?

How do those words sound to you?

LOOOOOOOOOOOOOOOOOONG?

BORING?

HOW A SAY WOULD ROBOT THEM?

HOW WOULD YOU SING or whisper them?

The plan for today is to...

PLAY

with the idea of
executive functioning.

And sometimes we'll call it EF for short.

What do you think that means?

For me, I am here to practice my
GOAL-DIRECTED PERSISTENCE!*
That means when I super intensely
want something, I'm all in!

*These executive functioning skill terms are credited to Drs. Peg Dawson and Richard Guare's EF framework.

Can you stay
with me though?

Let's try something called
BODY DOUBLING
to reach our goal.

This means doing
a task together!

Now, who are we
doing this with?

You're 1 of the bodies.

If you're reading with someone else, they're another body.

I'm a 3rd body.
(Flip to the author page. That's me!)

That's 2 (or 3) of us!
Body doubles for the win!

Did you know that you're helping my **sustained attention**?

By talking with me and hearing my story, I can focus on our topic: EXECUTIVE FUNCTIONING.

No, not rabbits. Not chickens.

EX-EC-U-TIVE FUNC-TION-ING.

What are you thinking about right now?

I just realized my thoughts were on **POTATO** chips. What?! I know!

What should I do?

Yes, you're right!
Think about...YOU!

Thank you. I'm back.

A confession though...

It took a lot to start this book.

That's called **task initiation**—
something my brain can
get **SO** sticky about.

Like gum, or honey...

What's the stickiest
thing you can think of?

I can do this.

But my brain just doesn't want to!

Try this with me:

BREATHE IN...

PAUSE.

BREATHE IN...

BREATHE OUT:

1, 2, 3, 4, 5.

OK. I know I can break this down!

What's the first, tiniest step?

HMMMMMMM
HOW ABOUT, TA

MMMMMMMM... LK WITH YOU?

Now, I am imagining what this book will look like when it's ALL DONE!

Whoo! That just gave me a boost.

I see myself writing this book—with you!

This is helping my **working memory**.

When I picture it, I can remember it.

Thanks, also, for your flexibility.

I know this book is...

WINDY, BENDY, AND A LITTLE UPSIDE DOWN.

A fist bump for your
response inhibition,
and not chucking this
book across the room
and running far, far away!

If you do need to do that...that's OK.

But next time, maybe try reading this...

IN A SWING?

IN A TREE?

OUTSIDE?

WHILE JUMPING?

That helps me.

Where was I?

Oh, right! Executive functioning!

So, I discovered something.

It's sort of a secret.

I want to tell you.

And then I want YOU to tell everyone you know. But only if you agree with it.

Are you ready?

I started thinking about *how* I think.
That's called **metacognition**.

Then I started experimenting.

I got curious.

I wondered aloud.

The people around me
started wondering aloud.

I noticed that when I'm hot,
sticky, tired, have sat too long,
am anxious, or thirsty...
my feelings want to

EXPLODE!

I wondered,

WHAT IF

I got ahead of my body
and brain's needs?

WHAT IF I opened a window, washed my hands right away, rested first, got outside, talked my feelings out, and drank a bubbly drink...?

Well, it turns out...

I feel SO much better.
I can think and feel my feelings
at that **JUST-RIGHT** level.

Not too much, not too little.

That's called **emotional control**.

Sometimes, we help ourselves.

Other times, we rally other people to help get us there.

That is totally cool. Don't let anyone talk you out of it!

We are here to help one another.

Say it with me.

Why are we here?

We are here to

HELP EACH OTHER.

At least, that's the vision I have.

The best kind of community
gives us space to voice how
we each need to live, learn, and

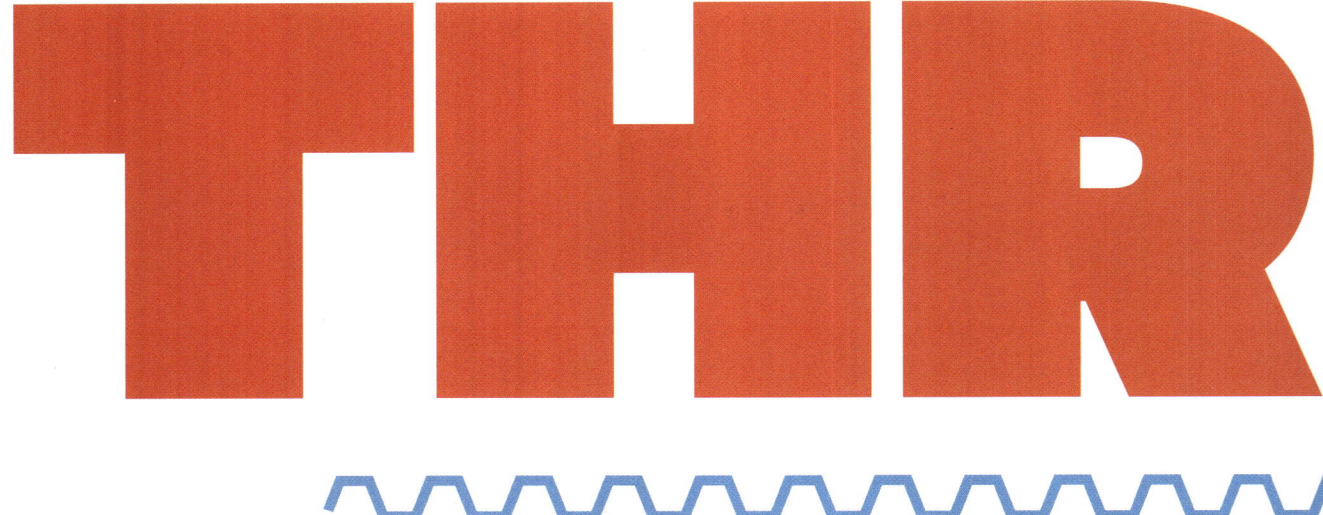

Different is not wrong, or less than.

Can you imagine a world where we celebrated all of our differences?

Now it's time for...
the **SECRET!** I almost forgot.

Working memory malfunction!

Onwards!

When all our brain and body parts talk, work, and play together (aka executive functioning), we can do...

ALL THE

THINGS!

Yes, the ones you want.

And also, yes, the ones your grownups want for you (maybe).

What do I mean by that?

I mean, if you've ever wanted to...

PLAN A TRIP, COOK DINNER, LEARN A GAME, FINISH A PROJECT, INVENT SOMETHING NEW, ORGANIZE YOUR TREASURES, BE ON TIME FOR A MOVIE, TELL A STORY, OR WRITE A BOOK

(P.S. YOU HELPED ME DO THAT TODAY! AWESOME JOB!),

all of that takes executive functioning.

Tell a friend.

Tell a neighbor.

Tell your pet.

And best of all,

HELP EACH OTHER.

Outro
for grownups

You made it! And now I wonder...what do you think about co-creating with our kids? Sharing your perspective, and really hearing theirs? This practice builds metacognition (a key EF skill!).

EF-building is an experiential way of supporting a kid in developing their autonomy, unique problem-solving mind, and recognition of who they are and where they want to go. Kids understand by watching and doing things with someone. That day you were really tired and couldn't think? Give them context (or they will make their own meaning). Let them see your gears turn and notice what restores you. Allow that reciprocation when they're the ones needing restoration.

Let kids in on your navigational process—how you care for your own brain and body—neurotypical or neurodivergent. You're helping them grow their language of executive functioning: naming, noticing what's easy, what needs support, or why they feel off on a given day.

This collective ability to articulate could create a powerful space for all our nervous systems to breathe, and for our diverse brains to be at their very beautiful best. Thank you for your curiosity.

About The Author

Iris Wong (she/her) wrote this book for her inner child, own kids, and anyone curious about the mind-body connection. A veteran of burnout, Iris has lived experience with the intersection of regulation, rest, executive functioning, neurodivergence, and societal expectations.

This book is a glimmery letter from one nervous system to another. Could 1 story and 1 wonder create a domino effect? This book was written to give us all language to translate what doesn't need to remain a mystery—how the brain and body work together—to help us uniquely thrive and connect. To help us name and notice our wiring and needs so that we can learn to give and receive, in real community.

 @eftoolkit   🌐 eftoolkit.com

Made to empower.

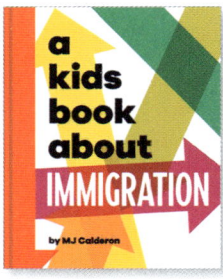

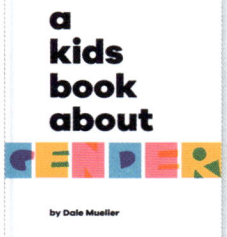

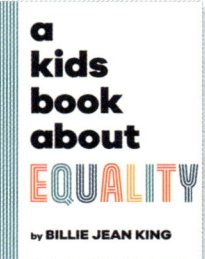

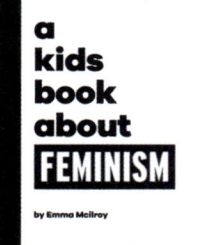

Discover more at akidsco.com